Biography of Benjamin Zephaniah

A Life Dedicated to Raising Consciousness Through Poetry"

Valerie A. Wood

Table of content

Introduction

Benjamin Zephaniah's journey from poor origins to becoming a renowned figure in literature and social movement is an enthralling story set against the backdrop of his upbringing and early life. Zephaniah was born on April 15, 1958, in Birmingham, England, and grew up in a challenging environment that shaped his distinct voice and worldview.

Zephaniah saw the intricacies of a society coping with racial tensions and injustice while growing up in the ethnically diverse Handsworth region. His parents, who had immigrated from the Caribbean, had firsthand experience with racism, which drove young Benjamin's zeal for social justice. His family and community's challenges became the crucible in which his devotion to elevating consciousness via poetry was born.

Zephaniah's childhood was not without difficulty. He was diagnosed with dyslexia and suffered academic difficulties, which led to his disengagement from formal education. This setback, however, served as a stimulus for his investigation of alternate avenues of expression. Zephaniah realized the power of words and their ability to transcend traditional limitations at the crossroads of adversity and creativity.

As a teenager, Zephaniah immersed himself in the colorful 1970s counterculture, enjoying reggae music, Rastafarian philosophy, and the developing punk scene. These inspirations would subsequently pervade his poetry, imparting a rhythmic cadence and a defiant attitude. Birmingham's streets became his school, and the people he met became his professors. This thorough education would become a pillar of his later work, adding authenticity and depth to his investigation of societal concerns.

The significance of Benjamin Zephaniah includes not just his literary accomplishments, but also his transformative impact on the perception of poetry as a medium for social change. Zephaniah established himself as a pathfinder, taking on the mostly white literary elite and clearing the way for poets of color to assert their voices. His relevance stems not just from his talent to write compelling verses, but also from his unrelenting commitment to utilizing poetry as a vehicle to combat systematic injustices.

Zephaniah's poetry became a platform for addressing oppressed populations' perspectives. His statements rang true, encapsulating the core of the difficulties encountered by individuals on the periphery of society. The review also includes his courageous investigation of subjects like racism, inequality, and environmental devastation, establishing him as a poet who is not afraid to address hard facts.

Furthermore, Zephaniah's importance is profoundly anchored in his function as a cultural symbol who transcends literary bounds. His use of poetry and music, particularly collaborations with reggae artists, broadened the reach of his message. This interdisciplinary approach broadened his audience while also emphasizing the interconnectivity of art forms in amplifying social messages.

Zephaniah's relevance in the context of British literature resides in his challenge to the established quo. He became a symbol of strength and resistance, inspiring a new generation of writers to break free from tradition and explore themes that reflected the many realities of modern society. Throughout his prodigious four-decade career, he not only carved a place for himself in the literary canon but also opened doors for others who, like him, sought to use their voices to catalyze change.

As we delve into the multiple layers of Benjamin Zephaniah's history and early life, we discover not only an individual's tale but the story of a generation. His significance becomes a testament to the transformational power of art, demonstrating how one person's journey may have far-reaching consequences beyond the bounds of personal experience. Exploring this poet of social justice's formative years takes us on a trip through the maze of identity, activism, and the enduring influence of words that reverberate with the cadence of change.

Chapter 2. Formative Years

Benjamin Zephaniah's early years were vital in turning him into the renowned poet and social justice champion that he became. Zephaniah was born on April 15, 1958, in Birmingham, England, and grew up in a multicultural neighborhood where he was exposed to a wide range of influences. This early upbringing sparked his interest in and love of the spoken word.

Early Inspirations and Influences

Zephaniah's early influences were diverse, relying on the rich tapestry of civilizations that surrounded him. He was raised in a largely Caribbean milieu, surrounded by reggae, dub, and the vivid oral traditions of the Rastafari movement. These influences' rhythmic cadence and strong storytelling made an indelible imprint on his artistic sensibility.

The poet frequently spoke about reggae music's influence on his early years, emphasizing its potential to express profound messages of resistance, identity, and social critique. Artists such as Bob Marley served as influences for Zephaniah's use of poetry as a form of expression and activism.

Zephaniah found inspiration in literature and the written word, in addition to musical inspirations. His ardent reading covered works by both classic and contemporary authors. The merger of these literary influences with his community's oral traditions laid the groundwork for his individual style, which is distinguished by a forceful blend of rhythm, poetry, and social relevance.

The Origins of Zephaniah's Poetry

Zephaniah's foray into poetry began in earnest during his adolescence. He began writing verses that mirrored the realities and challenges of his neighborhood, drawn to the power of words to impact change. Because of his Jamaican roots, the spoken word became a natural vehicle for him to share his ideas on societal concerns.

His early poems frequently addressed issues of identity, race, and the sociopolitical landscape. Zephaniah's comments were a response to larger themes of unfairness and injustice, as well as a reflection of his own experiences. His message was urgent, heralding the emergence of a distinct voice within the British literary world.

Participation in the "dub poetry" movement, a style of performance poetry that arose from the Caribbean diaspora, was a watershed moment in Zephaniah's early career. This movement gave artists a platform to use their voices as tools of societal critique. Zephaniah's performances, filled with reggae cadence and protest fury, struck a chord with audiences and established him as a singular literary force.

Zephaniah's poetry became a catalyst for debate and thought as he polished his art. His courage to embrace painful facts and challenge accepted standards distinguished him as a poet daring to explore the intricacies of human existence. This boldness, entrenched in his early years, would become a defining feature of his whole body of work.

Benjamin Zephaniah's early years were a kaleidoscope of cultural influences, musical rhythms, and literary ideas. These early experiences shaped a poet whose words would resonate with social justice, identity, and resistance. Zephaniah's journey began when he entered the arena of poetry, making an everlasting impact on the landscape of British literature and opening the way for a lifetime dedicated to elevating consciousness via the power of the spoken and written word.

Chapter 3. Literary Career

The literary career of Benjamin Zephaniah is a tapestry woven with strands of social consciousness, poetic genius, and a devotion to giving voice to the disadvantaged. Over four decades, he created a large corpus of work that appealed to readers of all ages. Zephaniah's pen danced across genres, from thought-provoking lines for adults to impactful narratives for teenagers and children, making an unforgettable impression on the literary scene.

I. Zephaniah's Literary Odyssey: An Introduction

Benjamin Zephaniah began his literary career with a love of language and a strong sense of social justice. His early works demonstrated a raw poetic aptitude that would eventually blossom into a diverse career. The arc of his literary production demonstrates his capacity to adapt his technique to a wide range of audiences.

II. Poetry for Adults: A Social Commentary Mosaic

Zephaniah's adult poetry is a potent combination of eloquence and advocacy. Through verses that challenge cultural standards, themes of racism, inequality, and the human condition reverberate. "The Dread Affair" and "City Psalms" are works that dive into the various layers of urban life, exposing harsh realities while delivering a ray of hope.

III. Building Relationships with Teenagers: Bridging the Generation Gap

Zephaniah effortlessly connected with youngsters as a poet in step with the times. His works for this audience, such as "Refugee Boy" and "Gangsta Rap," explored identity, belonging, and the issues that young people experience. He became a literary mentor, helping adolescents through the maze of adolescence with relatable characters and meaningful storytelling.

#4. Children's Literature: Sowing the Seeds of Wisdom and Imagination

Zephaniah's debut in children's literature is distinguished by a charming blend of whimsy and wisdom. "Wicked World!"and "School's Out: Poems Not for School" show his ability to captivate young minds while imparting valuable life lessons. His creative style and rhythmic lyrics create an enticing environment where learning is an experience.

V. Style and Substance Variation

The variety in both style and subject is one of Zephaniah's literary achievements. His mastery of the written word is demonstrated by his ability to fluidly segue between genres, from poignant poetry to fascinating novels. This variety not only expanded his following but also cemented his image as a literary giant.

VI. Zephaniah in Education as a Classroom Staple

Zephaniah's works became standard fare in English schools, complementing the educational experience with themes that struck a chord with students. His poetry was accepted by teachers as a means for generating debates about race, injustice, and environmental issues. Zephaniah became a teacher via literature, conveying not only knowledge but also empathy and social responsibility.

VII. International Impact

While anchored in the British literary scene, Zephaniah's influence was beyond national boundaries. His universal themes of fairness and equality struck a chord with readers all around the world, establishing him as a literary ambassador for social change. His works' translations enabled individuals from other cultures to engage with his messages, developing a sense of shared humanity.

VIII. The Evolution of Style: A Literary Journey

Zephaniah's literary development demonstrates his dynamic connection with language. Each stage of his career displays a growing understanding of storytelling, from the raw fire of his early poetry to the complex tales of his books. His eagerness to experiment with form and style piqued the interest of his audience.

IX. Verse Legacy: Beyond the Written Word

As Zephaniah's collection of work continues to inspire, his poetic impact extends beyond the written word. His influence on contemporary poets, especially those who advocate for social justice, is enormous. The spark he lighted for future generations of black writers continues to burn brightly, producing a literary landscape rich in different voices.

X. The Enduring Influence of a Literary Legend

Finally, Benjamin Zephaniah's literary career is a story of poetic talent, social concern, and a commitment to elevating the voices of the oppressed. His investigation of issues across genres has left an everlasting effect on literature, elevating him to the status of literary luminary whose words transcend time and reverberate with humanity's collective consciousness.

Chapter 4. Themes in Zephaniah's Poetry

Benjamin Zephaniah, a poet of note, used his pen as a strong tool to dive into the deep fabric of social justice issues. His four-decade writing career reflects a steadfast commitment to confronting racism, and environmental concerns, and a pioneering contribution to climate catastrophe awareness.

Zephaniah's poetry is an investigation of the human condition, with a strong desire for justice at its foundation. He confronted racism head-on, dissecting its foundations and revealing its poisonous expressions. Zephaniah presented vivid depictions of societal injustices in his verses, compelling readers to confront painful facts. His words were more than just an artistic expression; they were a call to action, encouraging society to demolish the systems that perpetuate racial injustice.

Another pillar of Zephaniah's lyrical attempts was environmental concerns. Zephaniah used his poetic eloquence to highlight the vulnerability of our earth at a time when ecological consciousness was only finding its voice. His words served as a rallying cry, imploring readers to acknowledge humanity's interconnectedness with nature. Zephaniah's environmental poetry was more than just observation; it was a call to stewardship, a passionate plea to protect the Earth for future generations.

One of Zephaniah's significant accomplishments was his early identification of the climate catastrophe. He integrated future environmental concerns into the fabric of his poems long before they became popular. Zephaniah's verses acted as a prophetic narrative, foretelling the repercussions of unbridled environmental plunder. His visionary stance on climate catastrophe awareness distinguished him, with his statements serving as a forerunner to the urgent global talks that would follow.

The interconnectedness of social justice and ecology is obvious in Zephaniah's poems. He recognized that these concerns were interwoven parts of a larger struggle for a just and sustainable world. Zephaniah advocated for a comprehensive approach to solving societal and environmental concerns in his poems, realizing that the fight for justice extends to the fundamental ecosystems that sustain life.

Zephaniah's investigation into social justice issues went beyond the written word. He used his position to actively interact with communities, boosting perspectives that were frequently ignored. His dedication to grassroots activity paralleled the issues in his poems, resulting in a symbiotic tie between his literary works and real-world advocacy. Zephaniah's poetry did not stay on the page; it poured into the streets, echoing in protests and movements for equality and environmental responsibility.

The impact of Zephaniah's work on racism and environmental issues was felt in classrooms across England. Educators noticed his verses' transforming power and used them as teaching tools to spark talks about social justice. Zephaniah became more than a poet; he became a vital component of the curriculum, shaping the viewpoints of future generations.

In the context of racism, Zephaniah's poetry served as a mirror, reflecting difficult facts, challenging cultural standards, and deconstructing preconceived assumptions. His verses prompted readers to confront preconceptions and argue for a society where diversity was not just welcomed but celebrated. Zephaniah's lyrics became a rallying cry for those on the fringes, demonstrating poetry's ability to elicit empathy and promote change.

In contrast, Zephaniah's environmental poetry was a call to environmental stewardship. His statements carried a strong feeling of urgency, pushing mankind to consider the implications of its acts. Beyond his poems, Zephaniah actively participated in activities and campaigns aiming at increasing awareness about ecological sustainability.

Zephaniah's insight has become increasingly relevant in a society coping with the environmental difficulties of the twenty-first century as a pioneer in addressing the climate crisis through poetry. His work reminds us that art has the capacity to go beyond its aesthetic worth and become a catalyst for social and environmental change.

Finally, Benjamin Zephaniah's investigation of social justice concerns, unwavering stance against racism, and pioneering contribution to climate catastrophe awareness through poetry have left an unforgettable impression on the literary and activist landscapes. His words continue to ring true, challenging us to oppose injustice, embrace diversity, and protect the environment. In a world that is still grappling with these complicated concerns, Zephaniah's poetry serves as a lighthouse, guiding us toward a more just and sustainable future.

Chapter 5. Impact on British Literature

Benjamin Zephaniah's influence on British literature is far-reaching, going beyond the words he wrote to mold the viewpoints of modern poets and the educational landscape. Zephaniah has made an indelible impression on both the literary world and the brains of people who connect with his work through his passionate and socially charged poetry.

The Influence of Zephaniah on Contemporary Poets:

The capacity to transcend conventional boundaries, uniting art with activism, is at the heart of Zephaniah's influence. His poetry has encouraged a new generation of poets to use their craft as a platform for change, frequently as a rhythmic and poignant reflection on social justice issues, racism, and environmental concerns. Poets now see Zephaniah's work as a striking illustration of how verse can be a powerful weapon for confronting societal concerns and pushing for genuine change.

Zephaniah's distinct voice, distinguished by its honesty and uncompromising attitude on subjects, has become a beacon for poets seeking to break away from traditional norms. His lyrics' raw vitality and sincerity remind us that poetry can be a dynamic force for reflecting the times and challenging the status quo. As a result, many contemporary poets are influenced by Zephaniah's courageous attitude, imbuing their own works with a similar feeling of urgency and purpose.

Integration of His Educational Work:

Zephaniah's influence extends beyond the realms of artistic expression to classrooms, where his poetry serves as a potent educational tool. His works are praised not merely for their literary brilliance, but also for their ability to engage pupils in important discussions about societal issues. Teachers include Zephaniah's poetry in their courses, encouraging students to think critically and empathically.

Zephaniah's poetry is an excellent teaching resource due to the accessibility of his language and the relevancy of his issues. Whether tackling racism, environmental degradation, or greater social injustices, his verses serve as a springboard for educators to engage pupils in discussions about challenging issues. Educators hope to foster a feeling of social responsibility and awareness in the future generation by embracing Zephaniah's work.

Zephaniah's influence on education extends beyond literature classrooms. His work fits into multidisciplinary studies, bridging history, sociology, and environmental science. This interdisciplinary approach teaches pupils about the interconnection of societal issues and promotes a comprehensive awareness of their surroundings.

Furthermore, the use of Zephaniah's poetry in educational contexts contributes to the diversification of the literary canon. Educators contribute to a more inclusive and representative literary education by spotlighting voices that may have been underrepresented in standard curricula.

Zephaniah's influence can be seen in the growing spoken word and slam poetry movements, in addition to formal education. Many new poets are influenced by his bold stage presence and ability to attract audiences, and many adapt parts of performance poetry into their own work. This dynamic movement in poetic expression reveals Zephaniah's influence not just on the written word, but also on the oral traditions that have long been an important element of literary culture.

Benjamin Zephaniah's influence on current poets and education is proof of poetry's transformational potential. Zephaniah has shaped the landscape of British literature not only through his fearless exploration of societal issues and unapologetic commitment to justice, but has also ignited a flame of inspiration that continues to burn brightly in the hearts and minds of those who follow in his poetic footsteps. His legacy lives on not only through the words he penned but also through the voices he inspired to speak out and make a difference in the world.

Chapter 6. Activism and Advocacy

Benjamin Zephaniah's life and legacy are intricately linked with a profound devotion to action and advocacy, using poetry as a potent vehicle to ignite change and raise awareness of important social concerns. This section delves into his involvement in many causes, demonstrating how he used his lyrical skills to affect concrete change.

A Strong Advocate for Social Issues:

Zephaniah demonstrated a strong devotion to exposing societal inequalities from the beginning of his creative career. His poetry was used to raise the voices of oppressed communities and shed light on structural issues. His early works explored the complexity of racism, inequality, and societal divisions, establishing him as a key player in the field of socially conscious literature.

Poetry as a Change Catalyst:

Zephaniah's poetry was a call to action, not just a reflection of society's ills. He was a firm believer in the transforming power of words and their ability to elicit empathy, stimulate thought, and, eventually, create change. He aimed to challenge norms, tackle prejudices, and motivate people to engage with the world critically through his verses.

Environmental Protection and the Climate Crisis:

Beyond traditional social topics, Zephaniah was a pioneer in using poetry to address environmental concerns. He used his work to raise attention to the critical need for environmental stewardship even before mainstream understanding of the climate catastrophe. His poems served as a sobering reminder of the interdependence between social justice and environmental balance.

Empowerment and Inclusion:

Zephaniah's advocacy was not limited to the written word. He actively participated in grassroots movements and activities aimed at building inclusivity and empowerment. He continually attempted to transform his poetic words into real activities that may bring about positive change, whether through public speaking engagements, workshops, or collaborations with like-minded organizations.

Education as a Transformational Tool:

Recognizing the transforming power of education, Zephaniah fought for his work to be included in the academic curriculum. He hoped to introduce pupils to storylines that challenged established assumptions and fostered critical thinking by doing so. His poems were not just a vehicle for artistic expression, but also an important educational tool for cultivating socially conscious minds.

Difficulties and Resilience:

Zephaniah's journey as an activist-poet was not without difficulties. His work, which involved challenging traditional norms and advocating for change, occasionally led him into conflict with existing institutions. However, his tenacity in the face of adversity and unshakable commitment to his ideas cemented his reputation as a role model for aspiring advocates.

Impact and Insight:

Zephaniah's influence on the activism and advocacy landscape cannot be emphasized. His ability to pour passion into his poems struck a chord with people from all walks of life, inspiring a new generation of poets, activists, and change-makers. His legacy lives on not only via the written word but also through the visible transformations in consciousness and attitudes that his work continues to stimulate.

Continued Importance:

Even after his death, Zephaniah's legacy continues to inspire individuals who use art and action to address societal imbalances. The enduring power of poetry as a tool for change is underscored by the continuous relevance of his teachings, which serve as a reminder that the written word has the potential to transcend its immediate context and inspire movements for years to come.

Also, Benjamin Zephaniah's activity and advocacy, as shown through his creative expressions, indicate a life dedicated to using words as a force for positive change. His journey exemplifies the persistent power of art in molding society narratives and challenging the current quo, leaving an indelible imprint on both literature and the pursuit of social justice.

Chapter 7. Recognition and Achievements

Benjamin Zephaniah's extraordinary literary career was adorned with countless accolades, honors, and extensive public recognition, confirming his poetry's tremendous impact on society. This investigation digs into the honors he got, the recognition he received, and the lasting mark he made on the literary landscape.

Honors & Awards:

Throughout his four-decade career, Zephaniah received numerous honors that recognized the depth and poignancy of his literary contributions. One of his most remarkable accomplishments was obtaining the Cholmondeley Award in 1999, a renowned award given by the Society of Authors to recognize excellent contributions to poetry. This honor recognized not only his poetic ability but also his lasting impact on the literary world.

Zephaniah's dedication to social justice issues in his art was acknowledged. The Walter Tull Memorial Prize, given in 2009, recognized his commitment to eliminating racial inequity. This honor echoed his unwavering efforts to raise the voices of marginalized groups via his poems.

His influence stretched beyond national boundaries, earning him international fame. Zephaniah received the Golden PEN Award in 2021, an honor presented by English PEN for a lifetime of great service to literature. This honor recognized his words' global reach and the enduring importance of his messages beyond the borders of his home England.

Public Recognition and Appreciation:

Zephaniah's influence extended beyond literary circles, and he became a public figure recognized for his dramatic spoken-word performances and passionate campaigning. His ability to captivate various audiences via both his written words and powerful live performances garnered him global acclaim.

The Queen's Poetry Medal, which Zephaniah earned in 2003, demonstrates the recognition he got at the highest levels of British society. This medal, bestowed by Queen Elizabeth II, recognized not only his literary accomplishments but also his poetry's greater cultural significance.

Aside from official recognition, Zephaniah's work had resonance in ordinary life. His poems became ingrained in the cultural fabric, being taught in schools across the country, ensuring that his messages of social justice reached future generations. This incorporation of his work into educational curricula demonstrates a broader recognition of his role in impacting talks about racism, the environment, and societal challenges.

The tremendous reaction he received at public appearances, poetry readings, and interviews demonstrated his work's ongoing popularity. Zephaniah's ability to communicate with broad audiences across traditional boundaries cemented his reputation as a poet whose words connected with people from all walks of life.

Legacy and Persistence of Relevance:

As we consider Zephaniah's prizes, honors, and public recognition, it becomes clear that his impact goes beyond the accolades themselves. His poetry is still studied, praised, and quoted, demonstrating the lasting relevance of his messages in modern conversation.

Part of Zephaniah's ongoing legacy is his influence on following generations of poets, particularly those from underprivileged areas. The attention he gained during his lifetime is both a recognition of his accomplishments and an encouragement for aspiring poets to utilize their voices to confront societal concerns.

Benjamin Zephaniah's journey through the realms of awards, honors, and public recognition demonstrates the transformational power of poetry. His ability to combine literary greatness with a genuine dedication to social justice garnered him not only respect within literary circles but also cemented his status as a public intellectual whose impact extends far beyond the written word.

Chapter 8. Personal Life

Benjamin Zephaniah's personal life was a tapestry woven with strands of familial links, nuanced relationships, and profound personal experiences. As a distinguished poet, author, and lecturer, he had the issue of blending his public persona with the purity of his private life.

Born on April 15, 1958, in Birmingham, England, Zephaniah's early years established the groundwork for his later investigation of identity, belonging, and human connection. Raised in a Jamaican household, he navigated the intersectionality of his Black and British identity, a theme that would resound through his poems.

Family played a crucial part in influencing Zephaniah's worldview and artistic expression. Growing up in a culturally rich setting, he drew inspiration from the oral traditions of his family, rooted in the rhythms of Caribbean storytelling. This familial influence became a wellspring for his creative activities, as he attempted to magnify the voices frequently silenced in conventional narratives.

Zephaniah's ties with his family extended beyond the domestic realm. His work typically delved into the broader concept of community, highlighting the interconnection of individuals in society. The poet's examination of familial and social bonds materialized in poetry that celebrated variety and challenged established standards.

In terms of romantic relationships, Zephaniah's personal life demonstrated a complexity mirrored in the intricate layers of his poetry. While details of specific relationships remain relatively secret, it is apparent that his experiences in love and partnership influenced his creative output. Love, in its numerous forms, became a constant topic in his work, addressing not only romantic love but also the love for people and the world.

Balancing a blossoming public career with the demand for personal privacy proved to be a tricky dance for Zephaniah. As his literary star soared, he wrestled with the intrusion of public scrutiny into his private activities. The paradox of being a public figure and a private individual drove him to ponder on the boundaries between the two spheres.

Zephaniah's commitment to social justice often spilled into his public character, blurring the barriers between the personal and the political. Whether addressing issues of racism, environmental concerns, or greater societal inequities, he displayed a rare honesty that resonated with audiences. This honesty, anchored in his personal views, allowed the public to identify with the man behind the poems.

Despite the challenges of public awareness, Zephaniah was intentional about safeguarding certain areas of his private life. The uncertainty surrounding his sexual relationships and familial dynamics added layers of fascination to his public image, keeping a feeling of secrecy among the spotlight.

The gap between public and private life reached a dramatic juncture when Zephaniah revealed his health issues. The diagnosis of a brain tumor eight weeks before his dying put his personal struggles into the public spotlight. In doing so, he not only acknowledged his mortality but also invited the public to experience a more vulnerable side of the acclaimed poet.

Zephaniah's ability to navigate the difficult balance between public and private spheres revealed the multidimensionality of his persona. While he embraced the position of a public intellectual, his commitment to preserve portions of his personal life represented an intentional attempt to protect the sacredness of intimate moments.

Benjamin Zephaniah's personal life was a rich mosaic, woven with the threads of family, relationships, and personal experiences. His career as a poet, campaigner, and individual was distinguished by a devotion to authenticity, both in his creative activities and the navigation of public awareness. The delicate tango between the public and the private revealed not only the man behind the lines but also the continuing intricacy of the human experience.

Chapter 9. Health Struggles

In a dramatic turn of events, Benjamin Zephaniah confronted a severe health struggle with the discovery of a brain tumor diagnosis. The revelation, released around eight weeks before his passing, sent shockwaves through both his personal and professional circles. This unanticipated surprise adds a difficult layer to Zephaniah's already multifaceted life.

The disclosure of a health problem of such scale obviously generated doubts about how the poet would manage this new stage. Zephaniah, famed for his bravery and unrelenting commitment to social problems, suddenly found himself confronting a personal battle—one that would test not only his physical strength but also his emotional and creative fortitude.

The impact of the brain tumor diagnosis spread throughout various facets of Zephaniah's life. First and foremost, the revelation spurred meditations on mortality and the impermanence of life. Zephaniah, who had spent decades penning poetry that addressed societal inequities and fought for change, now faced with his mortality in an intimate and personal way. This transformation likely influenced the topics and tone of his subsequent work, adding levels of reflection and sensitivity.

Moreover, the diagnosis unavoidably damaged Zephaniah's ability to engage actively in the public realm. The arduous nature of treatment and the inherent uncertainty of facing a major illness prompted a recalibration of priorities. The previously vociferous champion finds himself navigating a more private road, navigating the difficulties of health while seeking solace and support from those closest to him.

As with any health problem, the influence spread beyond the sufferer to touch the lives of family, friends, and fans. Zephaniah's disclosure generated an outpouring of sympathy and well-wishes from a community that had been moved by his comments. It also prompted talks about health awareness and the need of treating one's well-being, even for those who had spent their life advocating for the well-being of others.

In the sphere of Zephaniah's literary talents, the health issues brought forth a particular obstacle. Poets typically draw inspiration from their experiences, using grief and joy alike as raw material for their creation. In the face of a significant health problem, Zephaniah's relationship with his own mortality became a heartbreaking muse. His work during this period stands as a testament to the potential of art to transmute personal sorrow into universal expressions of the human experience.

The disclosure of the brain tumor diagnosis not only marked a chapter in Zephaniah's life but also delivered a deep lesson on resilience and the potential of the human spirit to create purpose even in the face of adversity. The impact on his art, while necessarily shaped by the realities of sickness, became a continuation of his legacy—a monument to his capacity to address adversities with the same courage and conviction that marked his poetic voice.

In short, the health challenges of Benjamin Zephaniah showed a new layer of his humanity. The public figure, recognized for his uncompromising dedication to justice, exhibited a vulnerability that resonated strongly with those who admired him. The interplay between his personal battle and its embodiment in his work serves as a painful reminder of the interdependence of life, art, and the enduring spirit of a poet dedicated to increasing consciousness via his words.

Chapter 10. Legacy

Benjamin Zephaniah, a luminary in the sphere of literature, has left an everlasting impression on the globe via his poetry, activism, and unshakable devotion to social justice. As we ponder on his legacy, it becomes evident that Zephaniah's persistent impact on literature reaches far beyond the confines of his own existence. His words, packed with passion and purpose, continue to resonate with readers, assuring the continuous relevance of his message.

Zephaniah's literary legacy is defined by a genuine dedication to expanding consciousness via poetry. His verses were not only a collection of words; they were a tremendous force that addressed cultural standards and fought rooted prejudices. By diving into the fabric of human experiences, Zephaniah developed a body of work that transcends temporal and cultural barriers.

At the heart of Zephaniah's ongoing significance is his ability to reduce complicated social challenges into heartbreaking lyrics that speak to the human condition. His investigation of racism, environmental degradation, and other important topics became a rallying cry for people seeking change. Zephaniah's poetry was a mirror reflecting the harsh facts of the world, forcing readers to confront hard truths and inspiring them to strive for a better, more fair society.

One of the primary components contributing to the continuing resonance of Zephaniah's work is its universal relevance. His poetry are not bound to a certain period or location; instead, they offer a timeless aspect that permits them to communicate to succeeding generations. The concerns he highlighted — racial inequity, environmental stewardship, and the human impact on the globe — remain important, ensuring that his message remains as urgent now as when he first penned his verses.

Zephaniah's impact on literature is further increased by his influence on modern poets. Through his powerful and unabashed voice, he cleared the path for poets of color to embrace their unique perspectives and speak openly about their experiences. His impact is not only visible in his own body of work but also in the voices he encouraged, underscoring the importance of varied tales in influencing the literary scene.

Beyond the written word, Zephaniah's legacy is inextricably connected with his activism and advocacy. His passion to social concerns was not confined to the pages of his poems but appeared in concrete efforts to impact change. Zephaniah used his position to amplify underrepresented voices and call attention to systemic injustices. In doing so, he established that literature is not merely a reflection of society but a catalyst for transformation.

The enduring relevance of Zephaniah's message is shown by its inclusion into educational courses. His work is not relegated to the shelves of libraries but is actively taught in classrooms, ensuring that fresh generations are exposed to his ideas and goals. By becoming a part of academic discourse, Zephaniah's poetry becomes a living monument to the enduring power of words to alter minds and inspire action.

Moreover, Zephaniah's legacy is formed by the junction between his personal and public life. His honesty as a poet and a person generated a connection with readers that transcended the page. His openness to discuss personal hardships, including his recent battle with a brain tumor, humanized him in the eyes of his audience. This vulnerability, paired with his perseverance, lends depth to his legacy, making it more sympathetic and profound.

The praise and awards conferred to Zephaniah throughout his lifetime further confirm his place in literary history. Awards serve not just as a testimonial to individual achievement but also as a recognition of the greater societal effect of an artist. Zephaniah's honors underline the importance of his work in molding debates and influencing attitudes, ensuring that his legacy is imprinted in the communal memory.

Benjamin Zephaniah's continuing impact on literature is a tribute to the transformational power of words when handled with purpose and passion. His legacy stretches beyond the limits of poetry books; it lives in classrooms, in the brains of aspiring poets, and in the collective awareness of those who strive for a more just and compassionate world. As we continue to battle with the challenges of our times, Zephaniah's words remain a beacon, guiding us toward a future characterized by empathy, equity, and the eternal legacy of a poet who dared to speak truth to power.

Conclusion

Benjamin Zephaniah's life was a tapestry woven with the threads of poetry, activism, and unshakable dedication to elevating consciousness. As we reflect on his journey, spanning four important decades, it becomes obvious that Zephaniah was not only a poet but a force for change, an advocate for justice, and a catalyst for societal consciousness.

In going into the subtleties of Zephaniah's life, one cannot miss the enormous significance of his early years. Growing up in a world that often neglected voices like his, he found consolation and strength in the written word. These formative years created the framework for a literary career that would not only mold his identity but also pave the way for future generations of poets of color. Zephaniah's journey was one of resilience and resistance against cultural standards, as he developed as a distinctive voice in the world of British writing.

At the heart of Zephaniah's literary undertakings is a commitment to understanding the subtleties of social justice. His poetry became a potent platform for addressing issues that plagued society, with racism and environmental concerns taking center stage. Through vibrant poetry and heartbreaking narratives, he probed the complexities of the human experience, challenging readers to confront hard truths. Zephaniah's contribution to the conversation on the climate catastrophe was pioneering, identifying him as one of the first poets to explain the environmental challenges via the lens of verse.

The power of Zephaniah's work reached far beyond the pages of his novels; it reverberated in classrooms across England. His poetry became a standard in school curricula, ensuring that the next generation imbibed the spirit of social responsibility and critical thought. Zephaniah, in this way, became not simply a poet but an educator, changing minds and molding ideas through the power of language.

As we reflect on his life, it is impossible to divorce Zephaniah's literary achievements from his role as an activist. His pen was not merely an instrument for artistic expression but a weapon against injustice. Zephaniah stood at the forefront of movements, contributing his voice to causes that sought equality, fairness, and a better society. His activism was not confined to the pages of his poems; it manifested in real-world activities and cooperation with like-minded persons and groups.

Recognition and awards interspersed Zephaniah's journey, highlighting the value of his work in the literary environment. Awards and distinctions, while confirming his talent, also acted as a tribute to the impact he had on readers and fellow authors alike. Public acclaim further strengthened his role as a cultural icon, a poet laureate for social justice whose writings resonated with various audiences.

Yet, amidst the praises and triumphs, Zephaniah stayed grounded in his personal life. The nuanced balance between his public persona and private experiences provided dimensions to the narrative of his life. Family, relationships, and personal challenges created a setting against which his poems gained depth and honesty. Zephaniah, the person, became as crucial to his legacy as Zephaniah, the poet and activist.

In the last chapters of his life, health issues cast a shadow over Zephaniah's journey. The announcement of a brain tumor diagnosis provided as a devastating reminder of the fragility of life. However, true to his indomitable nature, Zephaniah continued to interact with life and his profession, embracing adversity with courage and grace. The junction of physical issues and ongoing creativity became a monument to his tenacious spirit.

As we end our contemplation on Benjamin Zephaniah's life and contributions, his legacy stands as a monument to the transformational power of words. His poetry was not bound to the confines of paper and ink; it poured life into discussions, ignited movements, and sparked introspection. Zephaniah's life was a lived witness to the belief that art, in its purest form, has the power to be a catalyst for change.

In the annals of literature, Zephaniah's name will live as a light of social conscience, a reminder that poetry may be a formidable force for confronting the grave challenges of our day. His life, committed to raising awareness and encouraging action, makes an unforgettable effect on the literary and sociological environment. Benjamin Zephaniah, the poet of social justice, may have left from our physical reality, but his words continue to resound, encouraging us to confront, contemplate, and catalyze change in the world around us.

Printed in Great Britain
by Amazon

34333317R00035